THE DISAPPEARING ROOM

OTHER TITLES BY MARA BERGMAN

*The Tailor's Three Sons and
Other New York Poems*
(Seren, 2015)

Crossing Into Tamil Nadu
(Templar Poetry, 2016)

… *The Disappearing Room*
Mara Bergman

2018

Published by Arc Publications,
Nanholme Mill, Shaw Wood Road
Todmorden OL14 6DA, UK
www.arcpublications.co.uk

Copyright © Mara Bergman, 2018
Copyright in the present edition © Arc Publications, 2018

The right of Mara Bergman to be identified as the author
of this work has been asserted by her in accordance with
the Copyright, Designs and Patents Act 1988.

978 1911469 34 6 (pbk)
978 1911469 35 3 (hbk)
978 1911469 36 0 (ebk)

Design by Tony Ward
Printed in Great Britain by
TJ International, Padstow, Cornwall

Cover photograph by Mara Bergman

This book is in copyright. Subject to statutory exception and
to provision of relevant collective licensing agreements, no
reproduction of any part of this book may take place without
the written permission of Arc Publications.

Editor for the UK & Ireland
John Wedgewood Clarke

ACKNOWLEDGEMENTS

Thanks are given to the editors of the following publications in which some of these poems first appeared: *Acumen*, *Agenda*, *Ambit*, *Envoi*, *Internazionale* (Rome), *Mslexia*, *Oxford Poetry*, *Poetry Durham*, *Poetry East* (USA), *Poetry Nottingham*, *Poetry Review*, *Poetry Quarterly* (USA), *Smiths Knoll*, *The Frogmore Papers*, *The North*, *The Rialto*, *Writing Women* and the anthologies *Buzz*, *Pique* and *Solitaire* (Templar), *Not Only the Dark* (WordAid), *May Day* (Cinnamon Press) and *Tunnels and Bridges* (Gyldendal Uddannelse, Copenhagen).

A number of these poems appeared in *The Tailor's Three Sons and Other New York Poems*, winner of the 2014 *Mslexia* Poetry Pamphlet Prize, published by Seren, 2015, while others were written as part of a shared writing / visual art project called *Re:Collections*, inspired by the hidden collections at the Tunbridge Wells Museum and exhibited in the town's art gallery.

'The Summer My Father Died' won a prize in the Kent & Sussex Open Competition; 'East 13th Street *or* How I Met My Husband' won a prize in the Troubadour Poetry Competition; 'Saying Goodbye at St Pancras Station' won a prize in the Ware Poetry Competition; 'The Baby Doll' won the Kent & Sussex Folio Competition 2015. 'Inventory at the Apprentice House' was shortlisted for the *Mslexia* Poetry Competition 2017. 'Cream' was highly commended in the Plough Poetry Prize 2017.

The author's special thanks go to fellow poets Susan Wicks, Caroline Price, Mary Gurr, Clive Eastwood, Suzanne Cleary and Monzia Alvi, as well as John Wedgewood Clark, Tony Ward and Angela Jarman at Arc Publications and Amy Wack at Seren. Thanks, too, to Martin, Marissa, Eva and Jonathan, without whom many of these poems would not have been written.

CONTENTS

Inventory at the Apprentice House / 9
The Projectionist / 10
The Tailor's Three Sons / 12
Walking Iron / 13
The Photographer / 14
Stereoscopic / 15
The Photographer at Night / 16
The Photographer's Scan / 17
The Photographer Goes Skiing / 18
The Photographer Visits the Dutch Masters / 19
Edward Hopper on Long Island / 20
Waste Not / 21
The Summer My Father Died / 23
House of Innuendo / 24
Woman in Wells-next-the-Sea / 25
Judith's Paper Dolls / 26
Waiting for the Baby / 27
Otherwise Known As Barbie / 28
Girl With a Pen in Her Hand / 29
Cream / 30
The Part Fiona Played / 31
East 13th Street *or* How I Met My Husband / 32
A Quarter to Eight, New York Time / 33
"It's Too Late" / 34
Flight 800 to Paris / 35
Coming to England / 36
Castellain Road / 37
The American Group / 38
On Your Birthday / 39
Six Months Pregnant / 40
Bleaching of the Linen / 41
Extreme Degrees / 42
Freckle / 43
Instant Replay / 44

Six Children / 45
Wolf / 46
Garden Centre / 47
The Baby Doll / 48
The Broken Doll / 49
The Dispossessed / 50
The Disappearing Room / 51
Invocation / 52
Doll With Mended Face / 54
Conjoined / 55
Blackbird / 56
Leaving for France / 57
Feasting With Deirdre / 58
Goodbye, St Pancras Station / 59
Reflection / 60
Englishman in New York / 61
Trying to Kill Time at JFK / 62
Caff / 63
Doylestown / 64
Landscape / 65
Anonymous / 66
What We Do / 67
A Night Like This / 68
Lost Lake / 69
Lagoon / 70
Painting England / 71

Biographical Note / 73

INVENTORY AT THE APPRENTICE HOUSE
   Quarry Bank Mill, Cheshire

Sixty girls in all, ages nine to eighteen, sleeping
in pairs, one room crammed with thirty beds,
not a single fire but a window overlooking the courtyard:
one water pump, three privies with a bucket holding straw.
None would grow past four foot eight; worked twelve
hours in the factory, from six a.m., six days a week,
makes seventy-two, with a break for a dollop of porridge
in the right hand and not a single penny's wage
except for overtime (their payment guarded by the mistress
in her parlour), but room and board in lieu: a hot dinner
every night – potato and cabbage and twice a week, meat,
eked out with a bit more porridge. The factory may have shut
on Sundays, but church in the morning and church in the evening,
two miles there, two miles back is eight, then an hour
for lessons in the classroom, four long tables, eight long benches,
a sand tray, assortment of slates. Take away nine at least.
And their punishment for leaving? From three to seven days'
confinement and the forfeit of their fortune, often pennies,
sometimes pounds. When found, if a girl couldn't beg her way
to solitary, her hair was chopped off six inches.

THE PROJECTIONIST
    The Cinema Museum, London
      for Jack Noel

He was like Toto in *Cinema Paradiso*, the boy
who loved the pictures more than anything,
who, at fifteen, began the first
of five years as an apprentice
projectionist to James Donald of Aberdeen.

He can just about remember
the metal tickets and the Florodol
sprayed along the aisles to hide the smell
and disinfect; the seating indicator
so people waiting in the foyer knew

where they could find a seat when someone left
halfway through the film's continuous loop.
He still hears that call: "Light the carbons,
open the curtains, houselights off.
All right, Mrs Mitchell, let them in!"

And when one by one the houses closed,
the Castle and the Capitol, he bargained
for two lorry loads of projectors, reels,
sandwich boards and photo stills,
even the lavatory locks,

and brought them here, to the workhouse
where Charlie Chaplin lived. We watch films
in the meeting room, drink coffee in the chapel
while he uncovers a cinema sofa
that once lived in the foyer of the Rex

and for an encore brings out
swirling carpet squares from the Majestic,
a whole roll from the Ritz. Then, unfolding
a length of velvet and stroking it:
"Imagine what it was like to be there."

THE TAILOR'S THREE SONS
    The Tenement Museum, NYC

Nights I can't sleep, I think about the tailor's
three sons and how twelve people lived and worked
in a three-room apartment meant for four
when the Lower East Side was the most crowded place

on the planet. What was it they did? The cutting or basting
or sewing, right here, the finishing or pressing over there
while the clock's heavy ticking kept them sane, insane?
Afternoons they'd elbow through the teeming streets to catch

some air, some news, but after a long day, what else
to look forward to but a bowl of soup and then to sleep
on the red velvet sofa which looked, from a distance,
more lavish, and though cherished, was so narrow

it is hard to imagine enough room for even one young boy
to sit down. I think of the sons because when night came
at last, and the whirr of machines had flown out the window,
the clock's ticking rocking like a lullaby, they would

lay down their heads side by side on the sofa,
rest their throbbing feet on wooden chairs and lie, suspended,
to sleep the sleep of the young and the exhausted,
dreaming their immigrant dreams in thin air.

WALKING IRON

High above commuters clutching cardboard cups of coffee,
    stepping off curbs, losing hats to the wind, visible /

invisible as any angel among the clouds and spires, spikes
    and wire, floating on air amid the endless high-risers

a man walks iron, believing or not believing in the proverbial
    gift for heights, maybe simply striving to keep fear at bay

if only for his family hundreds of miles away across
    the border. His father's great-grandfather was the first

to leave *Kahnawake*, the Place of the Rapids, to work
    iron and build a bridge across the St Lawrence

and that man's son was first to boom out, to straddle air
    and girders, hoist beams and hammer.

Their nation built the Empire State, the Chrysler –
    hell, and the most magnificent Towers of all. And after

the disaster, passed on the baton to sons and nephews,
    nieces too, to dismantle the rubble, do what they could.

On Fridays he leaves his four-story walk-up
    in Sunset Park, Brooklyn, but not before stopping

at the Cheesecake Factory or his favourite Manhattan bakery,
    then crosses New York State to another country.

---

boom out – Mohawk expression for leaving the reservation to work in the city

THE PHOTOGRAPHER
for Ellen Montelius

She thought she would capture in photographs, one by one,
    the people in her town. Those of a certain age.
        Over a cup of tea she would make them feel at ease

in a room of their own, always immaculate,
    or maybe it was the light as it caught the panes
        and sills and ledges and made them gleam.

In the gold oval mirror, the face of a man
    in a bright-red jumper, his ghost-face, his double,
        and then you see him, fingers poised on the table

he uses for healing, while in an all-beige kitchen
    a man in dark glasses drinks coffee, his cane patiently
        waiting against a cupboard. Friends plays bridge

as they do every Wednesday, and through an archway
    a woman stitches on a black and gold Singer,
        maybe humming, maybe singing, and the only cat

sits on one man's lap by a bookcase of places he's dreaming.
    Between white spindles of a banister, a sister
        talks on the phone to her sister, each word miraculous

in its distance, and beyond a table set with a half-loaf
    or malt loaf, in a room that is not a room,
        a bright blue woman, an infusion of green.

STEREOSCOPIC

The photographer built a house
        out of leaf-mould
                from a stream bed,
then gave it a backbone
        so she could hide
               anything: feathers or bats' wings
or babies' teeth. She chose people,
        captured their image,
               then made a double.
Look through the viewer's
        thick lens, your eyes
                dance before balancing
on archway or doorway, light
        piercing windows or caught
                in a mirror, table edge, cup handle, hand
of a clock. As you focus
        a chair grows clearer, sharp
                as pain shooting through you
and someone familiar
        or a stranger starts rising,
                begins to walk towards you.

THE PHOTOGRAPHER AT NIGHT

    After the photograms of Susan Durges

The photographer worked outside, in the dark,
    with photographic paper
        and aluminium tray, she stood
in the river, held them under
    the surface of water, night
    her darkroom and her lover.
        Leaves sizzled overhead,
            stars exploding
over patterns
    of spiralling water,
        the tray growing heavier
as she positioned it
    exactly
    under spindly branches
        of trees in silhouette,
then paused
        to reconsider
bubble and ripple, foam and stick,
        the reliability of moonlight.
    An owl may have hooted in the distance,
a deer may have stirred
        while she knew
    and did not know when to flick
on the torch for a second
        of light – river-bed, river-stone, river-
            reed, whatever
leaf-branch hiss-of-night
    that by chance was captured
        without a lens, her camera
            the world.

THE PHOTOGRAPHER'S SCAN

He shows her the maps of darkness, puzzle
    pieces of spine, every light and dark
        crevice of her life.

"Your kidneys are healthy," he says,
    "your organs look good," then points
        to the lumbar spine – nerve endings dangling

like threads from balloons
    soaring to a grey dawn.
        "A beautiful view," he says, as if admiring

a valley from a mountain.
    She has always loved the honesty
        of black and white photographs,

and now these blatant truths
    scanned as she'd lain on a bed
        and was pushed through a tunnel

with her ears plugged, the cameras *click-click*ing,
    and at intervals someone asking
        Is everything OK? and

Most women find this relaxing
    as she tried to talk herself
        out of the panic she felt rising,

remembering the time in upstate New York
    she went caving. One of the passages
        was so narrow, she had to take her helmet off

so someone could push her through
    into a space so small she
        wondered if she'd come out alive.

THE PHOTOGRAPHER GOES SKIING

She's out of her element among this white –
  mountains of it – but it's where she's dreamed of being, here
    where the chairlifts disappear. And with a jolt she

jumps to a sheltered part of the slope, catches her breath and
  views the vastness of the Pyrenees and all around
    the swarm of skiers clearing paths with ease, dashing down

the mountainside, snow bright, sun bright on her face as she
  zigzags a descent that is … *exhilarating!* It's her second time only,
    she's not skiing really, but there's nothing to stop her
      trying, she knows

she can do it. And she does it – till something gives, there's a pop
  in her knee and it buckles. Maybe she's not injured, maybe
    there's no pain, so she tries but it wrenches again so

she rests as skiers pass, as she sits on her hands – they are freezing.
  And before she struggles to get up, to make the long
    descent by foot, she sees them: a woman sheltering her
      young child

between her knees, guiding her down the mountain's gentle curve
  while the man skis backwards facing them, a smooth dancer
    filming every movement, every moment.

THE PHOTOGRAPHER VISITS THE DUTCH MASTERS

She enters the National Gallery,
    then room after room to this room
of interiors, of whispered exchanges
    between richly dressed women

suffused in tangerine light. They knew
    how to make a small room spacious, guide the eye
to other places, life's brevity.
    A girl in blue

stands calmly by a virginal
    and a young boy, framed in a window,
watches a butterfly, a bubble
    about to burst. The photographer is drawn

to the table in a corner, to the finest
    surviving peepshow – a house that springs to life
when she peers through a hole on the side –
    those wine-red, blood-red velvet chairs, the walls

that realign to become a room
    leading to a room. Like the masters,
she loves perspectives, follows a door
    where light spills from a passage

with earthenware tiles, and through another
    where someone in bed is probably dying.
A woman wearing a wide collar
    reads beside her as a shadow passes

in a window. On the floor lies a letter
    for *Monsieur J. Hoogstraten a Dordrecht*.
When you cover the light
    everything goes dark.

EDWARD HOPPER ON LONG ISLAND

He left the neon-lit cafés and deserted stations
for a winter of snow, mounds of it,
steeped on decks through a neighbourhood
where he didn't know a soul.
He had given up city lights, city life,
to see the sun rise from a corner of a garden,
a flock of geese pummel across clouds.
At last the chance to study the filaments
of a squirrel's tail, the shock of red cardinal.
He'd go to bed later and later,
wake up earlier until
there was no discernible difference
between darkness and light.
Three a.m., looking out on the snow
when a plane passed over the row of split-
level houses, he spotted that thin divide
where streetlight met houselight – light
on the side of a building his favourite thing.
Maybe he wasn't so far from his life,
maybe it was here he stopped questioning
what he was doing amid the snowlight
and a pale orange glow
over the telephone wire, heat steaming.

WASTE NOT
    After an installation by Song Dong

From above, it is a cityscape of yellow stone
        infused with light – but moving closer
it's a market: every item neat and bleached in the sun,
then dabbed with colour, stacked on the floor
or aging cupboard, naked bedstead, old TV.

Closer still, it is a life: a treasure-house
        of plastic bottles and paper bags,
tins and vases, aerosol cans, bars of soap, fans,
peanuts in their shells: every *thing*
his mother ever owned.

Not a yogurt pot or plastic tray was thrown away;
bundles of newspapers, metal tabs.
Each birdcage, bedroll, bucket
a struggle to acquire.

Clocks. Lights. Soil.

To be frugal was a virtue.
She crammed her wooden home
with rusted pipes and slabs of greying Styrofoam,
empty toothpaste tubes and water coolers,
the nicks and cracks and chips of mixing bowls
her stories and her scars.
Buckles, belts, hangers,
protractors and coloured wire.

Every shoe her family ever wore.

To throw away her daughter's favourite doll
would be like rubbing out her childhood.
Her cuddly monkey will always be

about to crash its cymbals.
Pens, pencils, abacus.
Hair ties. Jump ropes.

Not a hint of silk or piece of jewellery
but one day
        she would free that brand-new tea-set
and lay it out on a table, sew the bolts of fabric
into vivid jackets, indulge in a pack
of Yun Yan Brand cigarettes.

The Family Excellent Ornament Co. Ltd duvet
is still encased in plastic, and the box
of Elegant Royal Mozart Chocolate
shaped like a violin.

The concept of *wu jin qi yong*, or waste not, was a prerequisite for survival in China in the 1950s and 60s.

THE SUMMER MY FATHER DIED

Boys stoned frogs the summer my father died,
surrounded the stream, there was never any hope,
and followed the floating white bellies.

My sister and I were left there, in Accord, New York,
in a bungalow swarming with cousins.
We wanted to be like them, unaware

of our steps as we ran through the dark grass.
Or of night's enormity – all those beautiful stars
forgotten above the wooden roofs.

Our aunts lived windows apart
and our uncles wore those white undershirts
with the scooped-out neck and arms.

On porch steps, as the orange light collected moths,
Aunt Dorothy kissed us goodbye, unable to answer
questions we couldn't ask.

HOUSE OF INNUENDO

I grew up in rooms of dark corners,
my mother slept with a knife.
Breakfasts were sliced with uncertainty.
I was hauled to school on a bus.

At night there was silence
or blasts of TV. I searched
for the man in the dark, prayed
for my father to come back,

heard cutting beyond the glass
of my room with two views: the house
of my best friend – her frantic semaphore
and lights – and our well-kept blooms.

WOMAN IN WELLS-NEXT-THE-SEA

Wearing thick black shoes, she steps straight out of the Bronx,
walks past the storefronts in her long white coat,

shuffling like my Grandma Eva along Olinville Avenue
when she'd take us to the candy store for bunches of lollipops

wrapped in polka-dots, or the playground's grey cement
with its stainless steel swings chained to the sky.

My sister and I called her every Friday before sundown –
Olinville 4-8033 – and saw her once a month

on Sundays, her building smelling of chicken soup,
the black and white tiles of her bathroom floor

shaped like lozenges, like chicken wire. One room
led to another in her railroad apartment by the El,

whole rooms shook when a train passed overhead
or the girl upstairs thundered on roller skates

across the living-room ceiling. My grandmother
hid twenty-dollar bills between pages of Dickens

she never read, one by one lost everything – country,
husband, two grandsons and then my father

and Uncle Harry, her sadness the swelling violins
playing "Tara's Theme" at the end of The Million Dollar Movie

each time we got ready to leave, everything turning black
and white, the bridge bathed in diamonds, the thick Bronx night.

JUDITH'S PAPER DOLLS

I used to confuse her with Anne Frank,
    my cousin Judith. Something about their smile
and dark eyes, the way their thick hair held
    so much life. I can still see her

in our grandmother's apartment
    writing words I didn't understand, later
folding sheets of paper and cutting out rows
    of children holding hands. For years – decades –

she went missing, the one and only cousin
    on my father's side, and after Uncle Harry died
she married an Italian boy and fled across the border.
    If only we had stayed in touch

we would be sisters now, releasing secrets
    behind doors of that narrow railroad apartment,
flooding rooms with light as each El train
    clattered past, rattling the windows.

WAITING FOR THE BABY

We played in Aunt Jean's living-room.
Cars passed, we peeked through white curtains.
Streetlights came on. We longed for home.

We wanted to lie in twin beds, side by side,
never to be alone in darkness,
our whispers slowly dying before sleep,

and a baby brother, the smell of talcum powder,
to dress him in tiny outfits.
We dreamed of tiptoeing to the next room,

watching the bundle of him breathe,
cradling him the way we did
our Thumbelina and Tiny Tears.

Our parents returned empty-handed and silent.
Soon all the little things were given away
and my sister's bed moved back.

Mom let us keep the perfect yellow robe
and at once it became our favourite.
We dressed our dolls in it.

OTHERWISE KNOWN AS BARBIE

It was love at first sight when Barbara Millicent Roberts
 arrived one winter in her shiny black case
  and a wardrobe teeming with colours and florals and fabrics

I'd never touched before: a silk-cotton sundress covered in tiny
 orange buds, the linen sailor dress with matching jacket,
  her pink mohair sweater. She carried an overnight bag

with leather handles, wore plastic shoes that fitted plastic arches
 exactly. Her calves slid under Capris, her breasts poked
  from crop tops and swim-suits and she came with

a ready-made boyfriend. She was doctor, lawyer, PA, vet, had an outfit
 for every occasion – and the most glamorous gold lamé number
  like my mother's. Most of all I envied her

her silk-black hair which she tied back
 in a ponytail, but if you undid the elastic band
  it was never the same. One spring, long after my friends

stopped playing Barbies and I knew better, I positioned her
 in our mimosa tree with its fronds outstretched and brimming
  with ballet-dancer flowers so she and Ken could do it.

GIRL WITH A PEN IN HER HAND

That Saturday I lay in bed, head throbbing,
throat on fire, my stepdad chose it
from the library, a biography

about three sisters who lived somewhere
in England. I loved to read
how they loved to write, I wanted to be

a sister like that. If it had been another day,
if I'd not had another throbbing throat…
I'm searching for it now, remembering

how I lay there turning pages
as the pain began to ease, releasing me
into winter on some windy heath.

CREAM

The coldest room in the house and the last he got just right.
He painted day and night, the walls a cool vanilla, so rich
it melted in your mouth, so smooth it dripped, singing
from ceiling and beams. A room to show off, a room
for dancing. He laid down an oatmeal carpet, then
travelled to the Carolinas with my mother
to find the perfect matching sofa and reclining chair,
cream through and through, down to the tender stitching.

It might have been the cream that killed him, ill so suddenly
he sank in it, thrashed as if in quicksand among the snake plants
by the sliding doors and a view of the snow-covered patio,
blinding in sunlight and milk-grey at dusk. Show tunes played
from the stereo, a vase held silver dollars my mother had grown
and dried while the oak-cased clock unticked under metal ferns.

THE PART FIONA PLAYED

She lived down the corridor, or we thought she did,
but maybe that was only DeLea. He was older,
wore glasses, his voice was high pitched
and they partied to Springsteen at all hours.

Littell Hall, Oneonta, New York, and this girl
from somewhere in England.
She wore skirts that flounced when she danced –
and she always danced first, had every boy swooning

though DeLea had already nabbed her.
We never really spoke, but she was my first
English person up close, fitting in
without even trying. She skipped classes, was always

hung over, but things somehow went right,
her accent gloriously spilling
while the rest of us struggled with work and love,
the long winter days full of snow up the hill,

hair freezing those nights after swimming, arms aching
with loss. Last I heard she was living in California
and never looks back.

EAST 13TH STREET or **HOW I MET MY HUSBAND**

If Aunt Dorothy and Uncle Seymour had moved
    out of their two-bedroom apartment with my four cousins
as planned, I never would have met Susan Silver,
    who lived in their courtyard, Utopia Parkway, Queens,
and grew up with Sharon and Tara, and years later
    I might not have known her at university
or become best friends, lived together in that red semi
    on East Street next to Feeney's Fine Foods and Drink
with Marla, the actress who spent weekends in New York City
    with a jazz musician twice her age. The three of us
ate only with chopsticks at a cable spool we used as a table,
    visited Dunkin' Donuts in the middle of the night
and found, once, a star on our receipt and won
    another dozen. We lived up the street from Mary and Albert
with their parakeets Sonya and Raskolnikov, and Peter, the potter,
    who borrowed my Brother typewriter to write a book
on Abstract Expressionism. I would never have heard
    that Susan met an English guy that summer while camping
with her boyfriend in Vermont, that he would borrow a sleeping bag
    and have to return it. She would not have rung me up
to join her in Manhattan, and I would not have said no and
    she would not have cajoled me until she convinced me to go.
I would not have seen him standing in the doorway
    of his friend's apartment on East 13th Street and thought *Yes*.

A QUARTER TO EIGHT, NEW YORK TIME

A quarter to eight and the sun streaming in.
    In my life across the Atlantic, the day half gone already,

my children having lunch, the light a little stronger.
    Here, I have no children, husband, house, no work

to go to. I wear jeans ripped at the knees, my hair's unruly
    and I'm for ever dreaming of someplace better.

On my shelf is an oversize paperback, *Vagabonding in America*.
    I read it every night, sleep in an orange mummy bag

I haven't yet shared, my windows open to the whistle of trains
    heading west. I plan to cram the things I can

into the bicycle panniers I made from a Frostline kit
    and cross America with a friend I haven't yet fallen in love with,

who won't be the one to leave me on a corner in New York City.
    That rush of cars up the road in the rain

is always with me. Seventeen and full of hope,
    heading somewhere.

"IT'S TOO LATE"

Boats are lapped by the harbour
as we aim for the sun. Through sandals
the pavement pulses, every part of me
on fire. The smell is fish just caught,
still flicking, the air so purely
sea, this song so clearly seventies
playing from restaurant speakers.
    I've no idea
whether something is beginning
but as we walk towards the end
of the pier, our shoulders rubbing,
I am treading whole oceans
and choose not to hear
the words the singer is singing.

FLIGHT 800 TO PARIS

I wake to news of fireballs
breaking the sky, the sea a swell of smoke,

and I think of my parents on Long Island,
stepping out on their deck smelling disaster –

smouldering fuselage, cloth, skin.
I think of me packing in the basement

the summer I came to England,
forcing my belongings into the two cases

for the journey. The room was cool,
the freezer hummed and the light was the grey

of the ceiling, oppressive and secure. Outside,
grass browned, and from the moment of take-off

emerged a new beginning. I think of those students,
and their parents daring to watch, proud

and full of fear, as they packed while practising French,
already feeling a difference in themselves.

COMING TO ENGLAND

After I unpacked, full of jetlag and timelag and fatigue,
I walked along Lewisham High Street for my very first
cup of English tea, the next day took the tube to Hampstead Heath

to visit Keats. Mornings I woke to the clink of milk,
and once a week the rattling rag-and-bone-man's cart, at first
not knowing what I was hearing as it made its way down the road

along the park, our slice of country. I spoke of "Lie-ses-ter"
and "Tra-fal-gar", went to the theatre for 50p and sat
in the heavens, queued up with the others to call home once a week

used a hand-held shower to save water, pointed to cress
in the refectory and called it clover, laughed at
toad-in-the-hole and spotted dick. Back home at a party

someone had told me you could buy a single cigarette
at an English market, even a match, and that I couldn't leave
New York City until I'd read *Return of the Native*.

CASTELLAIN ROAD

Bright pink door and white steps up
    we thought we'd finally made it, an address
        in Little Venice and a stone's throw from the canal,

our one room vast, with accordion doors
    that hid a kitchen sink and shelves of crockery.
        The loo down the hall was never clean, the bathroom

two flights up, our fridge the window ledge
    that overlooked a park, always locked.
        We lived on taramasalata from the Turkish deli,

good bread, yogurt, and tea, tea, tea; we travelled three
    tube stops away to work split shifts, night shifts, long shifts.
        Days off I sat on a grassy hill while ducks paddled

by canal boats as I read or wrote
    copious letters, homesick and worksick – until I met
        the steeplejack, said *No* but followed him

in the news when he scaled Nelson's Column,
    slept restlessly in the middle of that room
        between synthetic sheets, the one-bar fire blazing.

THE AMERICAN GROUP

Some of us have been here long,
some of us are only just unpacking.
Between us we could fill a bus with children
though some of us do not have any children.

Some of us speak the language with an accent
very much like English, but not exactly.
One of us is half French, and two
come all the way from Hawaii.

All of us have different
ties to New York City. Childhood summers
spent somewhere in the country, marriages
that brought us overseas

to become who we wanted to be.
But deep in our throats words stick
like a wishbone. We may have adopted "car park"
but what we're dying to say, really,

is "parking lot", recalling those
expanses stretching from store to store
and all the way to the beach
those nights in summer.

ON YOUR BIRTHDAY
   for Marissa

You weren't born yet, six years ago.
    Just past midnight, you thrashed inside me

as I paced and writhed like an animal
    struggling in the desert. Later, you proved unwilling,

held back in the dark while I pushed and pushed,
    reliving the Grand Canyon – hiking to the bottom,

not a single star that night, then two days' rain
    as we slogged and slid through mud and mule shit,

every muscle straining, hating every minute,
    following blindly those endless switchbacks out.

SIX MONTHS PREGNANT

Behind the door to your mother's room
the flies buzz like helicopters gone haywire.
Slower than summer, thicker,
they cut into the yellowing walls,
the cobwebs hanging like torn lace.
I'm glad she'll never see this.

This room smelled of powder
and bottled perfume on a Limoges tray.
She hated the grinding of wings,
would bend in her red velvet chair
for the swatter, slap curtains and table,
whatever she could reach, till the end.

I pick up a worn brown sock
and strike, pinch them till they pop
and drop to the carpet. I'm tired,
it's nearly one, but around the light
the buzzing multiplies as if they are
breeding under this false sun.

BLEACHING OF THE LINEN

October light red-gold through the trees.
I had forgotten this, having been away so long.
I hang out the wash –

two dozen terry-cloth nappies
evenly pegged, slightly sagging along the edge,
a configuration of flags swaying over grass.

It is wasted effort; it gives me pleasure
to have them dry in the sun, maybe
for the last time. I stand back and look

as though something has been accomplished, as though
this arrangement of squares deserves admiration,
just as once I stood and gazed

at a painting called "Bleaching of the Linen",
white sheets catching light
before being folded away.

EXTREME DEGREES

It was the winter of fearing water,
of not drinking from the bedside glass,
of forced showers, dizzying in the bath.

It was the winter of scorching snow,
of walls pressing closer,
my heart frantically breaking away.

It was when our fingers froze
on the steering wheel, our mouths burned
on hot cheese, when I looked in the mirror

and saw ash. Of the eyes I asked
How could you? Frostbitten wires
sizzled with whoever would listen.

FRECKLE
   for Eva

When I lifted you out of the car seat
and caught the edge of your pink-checked trousers,
I noticed your first freckle, just below your knee,
almost round, a slight pale seed, hardly there.
I look for it every day now – touchstone, landmark –
as if to make sure you are mine, watch
as you grow. You will wear it all your life
and I will always remember that first glance
on the way to the zoo. How you cried when we left
the elephants, how your sister kissed you.

INSTANT REPLAY

for Jonathan

It is the image of my two-year-old son
and his open smile that allows anyone to enter the world
of his innocent mouth, of his pure white teeth, the way
he runs with his knees high and his arms all over
wearing his alphabet sweater, with row
after row of *house, cat, boat*
knitted in primary colours, the image of him running
nearly within reach as I fumble for my keys and then that step
that takes him closer and the flash – *red* – the space between
his beautiful, perfect head and the glass window
of a shiny red car that is going too fast just as he
is going too fast. I lunge and grab, fingers piercing wool
as the space widens until it fills the car park, the horizon
and the car is far away, over the mountain
of ramp, out into some sunset on a strip of desert
and here, in my arms and laughing, is my boy, my boy.

SIX CHILDREN

I could not do it and laugh, ever,
or last to the end of each day,
one gnawing my elbow, another limp
round my neck, bruised toes, squashed hip.
Where would we put them, how
would they fit in the car or the kitchen
and how many beds? I fear for my life
as it is. Look, my hands
are wearing away. If I had six children
would they eat their peas?
Brush their teeth? Would they ever sleep?

WOLF

If I think of him as dog
he won't harm us. His thick tail
dusts the stairway, brushes the walls
as he steals into each room, searching,
waiting for the first sure chance
to catch us off-guard, for the children
to call him his wrong, adopted name,
for them to say it, *dog*, so he can have them.

His fur is unbearably soft, see
the dense white of it, a snowstorm tinged
with night. For an instant I am caught
in the spell of his smooth stride,
imagine my fingers sinking.
His teeth are sharp white.

I should have noticed him before
lurking in the park behind some tree,
crouched between the rows of runner beans
in my neighbour's garden. I could have studied
his shadow, seen how it rested
on brick, distorted on corners, quickened, pounced.
I should have tried to know him,
observe him sleep with his snout
buried deep in that magnificent tail.
I should have trapped him.

Maybe it's not too late.
As I let him smell the carpets, rub
against the innocent legs of my children
he needs to discover for himself
it is not us he wants, we are the ones
he chanced upon, we are just anyone.

GARDEN CENTRE

We sidestep the last mounds of snow
to where it is spring – the first crocuses and irises

potted and luminous, row after row of luscious packets
boasting *Little Marvels, Autumn Kings, Scarlet Globes.*

As if this isn't proof enough, there's a rainbow full of ice pops
already in the freezer. I buy my daughter a Zoom, purple

dripping as we walk outside, past tables of heather – *Ruby Glow,
Orange Queen, Golden Carpet* – to the sheds and conservatories

by the wood, to the house with gingerbread shutters, bay window,
real glass. "That's where the Three Bears live," says my daughter.

Beyond azaleas and the thin hard promises of roses
we play visiting. Two red chairs reach my knees, the top step

my giant's eye-level. She is no longer little
in this house, glad to see me and yet unsure. When we hug

hello, I want to shower her with all the colours
I have gathered, but all I hold are a few small heathers.

She places them in the window, slowly, deliberately,
as though she is lighting candles – her *Spring Torch, Pink Star.*

THE BABY DOLL

This is where they come to rest.
Sixty thousand objects hidden here
under the museum floor: balsa wood temples

from India, peepshows and panoramas,
magic lanterns and random pewter,
costumes, soldiers, a giant turtle.

We ease a box down from its shelf and
navigate between aisles of optical instruments,
buttons and birds' nests. Ephemera.

On a table in a patch of light we lift the lid:
a baby doll dressed in a soft pink sweater
with white buttons and cuffs.

Her sleeves are empty
where her missing arms should be.
A silk ribbon holds her leggings up.

We had an unwell baby once, a baby doll,
a brother. He slipped away in hospital,
sailed to sea in a boat. We never even saw him

and there weren't any tears
but we loved him. Inherited his outfits.
Dressed other babies in them.

THE BROKEN DOLL
    Early nineteenth-century bisque doll

Let's put the baby together.
All the components are ready,
the pale wide forehead and dimpled chin,
a porcelain-perfect skin you want
to smooth your fingers over. Cheeks flushed –
she's been in the sun, laughing at trees, smiling
at some little-girl mum – orange lips
too old for her years, a two-toothed baby smile.
You can just make out her tongue.

Each hair of her eyebrows and lashes
is expertly painted, but let's fix the eyes,
unlooking, unseeing, rolling like blinds.
Let's clean out the darkness of lids.

How shall we dress her, this baby doll,
this girl? One fine-stitched dress to cover
her blue-tinged limbs and belly,
a pair of knitted socks and polished shoes
to shelter those curled, chipped toes.
A wide-brimmed hat to protect her.

THE DISPOSSESSED

    After a collection of early nineteenth-century dolls-house dolls

Now more than ever I think it was fire
yet the butcher still brandishes his pick
and cleaver, wears his apron's collection of stains
down the middle. His hair, black and thick, enticed women
to run fingers through it, clasp his big meaty head
to their bosoms. Under treasured pearl buttons
dark stitches jut like bones.

Was it Madame or was it her sister, one wearing purple
the other blue velvet? The daughter seemed likely,
her arms wooden and clumsy – miniature rolling pins, hinged
at the elbows – her sleeve ripped at the shoulder as if
someone had grabbed her blood-claret dress
which would never shimmer. The favoured aunt,
maybe? And what of the butler?

Did he fancy the maid in her Swiss-dotted dress
though her sweater was fraying? Or the maid in pink roses?
Surely the children saw everything – from first flirt
to courting to flames growing higher. Were they jealous
of their cousin, so much younger and sweeter,
in her favourite blue dress with the wide ruffled collar?
And was it the spaniel who toppled the candle

and sent the rooms spinning as fire ripped
through the curtains? Not one of their hairdos was mussed
in the mayhem, the dark waves remaining
flat on their heads. Now all is calm and, though roomless
and homeless, they rest in these nests of crisp tissue,
contented. Except for the maid in her red-spotted dress,
her arms outstretched, still raising the alarm.

THE DISAPPEARING ROOM
South Florida Science Museum, West Palm Beach

See her in the empty room
with the skirting-boards rising
into wallpaper sprouting with flowers.
Not a chair is in sight as she slides
from corner to corner in a slow motion
she's grown accustomed to.
People have been stringing her along for years
with her bead-black eyes
and her apron of patches on patches,
clean and neat, sewn with the finest
stitches. They flock to visit.

Her feet never touch the floor.
She's a small child, a baby doll,
and shrinks as she moves away
while the room takes on life
and grows before our eyes. She returns
because we want her to, because we pull
the strings. She heads towards centre
as if towards some natural disaster.
We are doing it and cannot free her.
And she does it again because we do it again
and as she moves into the corner
the room is disappearing.

INVOCATION
    After a photogram by Adam Fuss

When she places her baby
    on the paper
        and I shine the flashlight

his arms splay, his legs
    bow, but
        not a cry.

I had always thought
    my best work
        was done – the ghost dress

with its beads
    of neon lace-lights
        shimmering

in a dark dance,
    or the ladder simply
        reaching –

but this baby emerges
    amphibious, an orange
        phenomenon rising

from volcanic yolk.
    Chance
        captured the tiny crevices

of his neck and bottom,
    curve of nose,
        and along his left side

his outline an exact pen line,
    I couldn't have hoped
        for anything

more spectacular,
    shadow-spine and sea
        urchin along his side,

those whispers
    of hair.
        See him   crawl   swim   fly

DOLL WITH MENDED FACE

Though my sister's beautiful limbs were ruined
    her face is unscathed, while mine is immediate proof:
rivers cross and cross my cheeks and the bridge
    of my nose to meet and pool in one eye.
        My mouth is not my own, nor my teeth.

The surgeon made no promises
    as he shifted sections of my face
like tectonic plates. Nine months old.
    We remember nothing, though at night
        we flinch at any shadow.

My mother saved the news-clippings
    for when we grew up. She'd lull us to sleep
with stories of another time, a time *before*, never saying
    the words *dragged* and *mauled*, *struggled* and *bloodied*.
        Bruises. *Torn*. Not once did my father repeat *Babygro*.

CONJOINED

> Jodie and Mary were born August 2000,
> St Mary's Hospital, Manchester

Two babies in one, fused
at the spine, joined at the abdomen,
their limbs ram-
rodded at right angles.

And then in less than a day
the surgeons separate
bone and flesh, a body
from its heart and magically

the girls are free, apart
for an instant
before one is able to live
without having to pump blood

for her sister, breathe
for her sister, drag
her sister's body.
Through little tricks she will

survive. The first: to ease
the strain of being alone,
one cold mirror
propped in her cot, beside her.

BLACKBIRD

Two years back, a blackbird
would alight on our roof, mornings barely beginning

to turn from black to grey. And it would call
with that full-throated, slightly grating song it had,

upbeat and soaring across grass and fields, impatient
to bring on day. I felt less blessed

last spring when not a single blackbird came
but chose next door. I woke with it at dawn

to watch it from our skylight in the hall.
A silhouette – mechanical, still as tin –

and then that beak – more parody than real,
movement somehow not quite matching sound,

the sound too much a melody for those
staccato moves. And this says nothing

of the body underneath all that
opening, shutting, opening –

steadying the roof and lifting the sky.

LEAVING FOR FRANCE

At three a.m. you walked out the door
with your one small suitcase. Streetlights
blinked as you headed towards the park, your steps
hissing to the stars. You met your connection
by the station and drove to the coast
as mist lifted, and when the boat left
you were free. As you sat in a café

with paralysed contentment, alone
savouring baguettes and brie, imagining
the evening celebration, or in the morning,
moving through the marketplace as croissants
rolled hot off paper sheets, did you think
you could make your life again, miss the boat
day after day to begin here?

FEASTING WITH DEIRDRE

More than anything, I long to take you out to lunch!
To Bellamy's, just along the Kennington Road.
We could stop in at the city farm first,
visit the chickens with stacks of feathers on their heads

like wigs, or helmets, and oven mitts covering their spindly legs.
We could enter the church's garden for a minute's silence
to remember Margaret, then step into the glaring sun
before dodging into an alleyway as if we were in Jerusalem

or Paris, and slip through the doors of the deli.
Over the counter, platters of blushed tomatoes and aubergine,
seas of baby leaves, goat cheese, grilled vegetable quiche.
Our mouths will be watering and I'll lean over

and say, *Choose anything. Everything!*
believing in all of those colours, that goodness.
Your skin will radiate health,
your hair grow back long and shining and sleek.

GOODBYE, ST PANCRAS STATION
> Listed in *The Independent* as one of the most romantic
> places in the world

Of course, one of you must be leaving
for someplace far, and north,
and of course it must be night, preferably
clear and cold, a hint of snow.

You'll wear thick coats, scarves, gloves,
and the station will feel cavernous,
the boards swelling with departures –
destination after destination pressed together

with his, then all those arrivals
you can't look at. You check your watches,
there's time for a coffee, so you sit in the chrome
and the warmth, huddled in a corner

the flush of his neck under a sweater, your
frantic heart. It won't be long now, you're savouring
every sip, every second, but when the time comes
you'll do it right: he'll lean out

over the window and you'll look up –
you can see it. Along with the tears
and the sadness, one long last lingering kiss,
the train struggling to pull away.

REFLECTION

The man in the train
leans into
the woman on the platform
in her blue suit.
She is reading the paper.
He wears a plaid shirt,
worries his hands,
turns them and turns until
they grasp her shoulders,
smooth her arms and clasp, at last,
her hands. He dips all his body, his head,
and somehow, despite everything –
light on shadow, transparent on opaque,
the way they are travelling
in opposite directions and the day
is dying on the tracks –
their mouths find each other, kiss.

ENGLISHMAN IN NEW YORK

You rescued him from the dark
    subway platform as a train heading downtown

pulled into the station, he was something rare
    you wanted. Your fingers lit his elbow

and guided him in. After that, dinners in Little
    Italy, India, Korea, then his apartment,

its furniture and walls all beige, with dozens
    of photographs, he described every one, painting

the ideal English childhood before his eyes
    clouded over. His acute sense

of order, the shirts and ties and suits
    coordinated in his closet, one drawer for blue socks, one

for black, his fingers caressing every surface, expert
    at wielding a knife. At night his accent

cut the New York City air, *Why have a dog*
    when a stick would do?, and with it he tap, tap

tapped into your heart. When you made love
    his eyes were utter blue.

TRYING TO KILL TIME AT JFK

I am earlier than I've ever been before, for anything,
breeze through check-in, am free
to wander the concourse of duty-free and places to eat –
Wok 'n' Roll, McDonald's, muffins at Ritazza, sandwiches
at Au Bon Pain, and gallons of coffee, coffee everywhere,
as if caffeine were the secret ingredient of flight.
At the Museum Shop, I study calendars, mugs, keyrings,
imagine a stranger begging me to choose something –
and without hesitation, I'd point to the citrine earrings
under glass with their fine Victorian clasps. One whole hour
at Hudson Bookshop perusing dedications, measuring
what I haven't read, then comparing candy displays
at Hudson News among hundreds of magazines.
*What could be better than having a back massage
at the Xpress Spa?* I visit the bathroom every half hour,
check my hair, redden my lips, drink from the taller
of two water fountains before standing by Longchamps
    Luggage and Handbags,
before going outside into the air of New York City
one last time to watch a sparrow, listen to traffic on wide lanes
for what might be a very long time, for what may be for ever.

CAFF

I used to love these places: the secretive grey
net curtains, the smell of grease, unshaven
men in flannel shirts, and blue, and smoke.

In small towns, in winter, walking streets
and never feeling warm, trying to fill
a certain emptiness and being drawn

to broken bricks and splintered doorways.
I come here now for the milky sweet coffee
that lets me imagine I'm at home

in some other country, having perfected
the inflections, getting the accent right,
counting out my change to the penny.

DOYLESTOWN

Sometimes I think we should have stayed there
and gone each week to the local cinema
where we'd watched figures on a distant screen
go about their lives, frame by unhurried frame,
knowing exactly where they were headed
while we huddled in our velvet seats
and dipped blindly into buttery mounds of popcorn.

At the museum of local history, ploughs were suspended
from the rafters, horse-carts, sleighs, as if a tornado
had not yet set them down or the drivers had left
in the middle of a snowstorm to warm their feet
by a fire. Everything there – the bottles and tortoise-
shell combs – said, *People have lived here
all their lives, rocked on white porches in summer,
stared through long frosts for the first signs of spring.*

I would gladly sit at the coffee shop on the corner
where we'd squeeze into a table to the whirr
of a milkshake machine; line up at the newspaper shop
on a Saturday night for the Sunday *New York Times*,
caught in a net of half-dream and half-truth, believing
in Main Street, USA, where everyone knows everyone
and each clapboard is inextricably in place.

LANDSCAPE

The language of this landscape is sugarbeet,
thick, white, with fine concentric circles
that dare you to bite into centre; it's

the deep sea of cabbages stretching to
farmhouses saturated with light,
red brick, Dutch gable, wingbeats of gull; it's

a crossroads of villages nothing more
than clustered houses, gravel paths, a splash
of red on a pole. Tractors navigate fields.

And the weather of this language is calm,
endless as sky. At night we sink into velvet,
cut off, in the dark, on the fringe.

ANONYMOUS

First I must know
if I can be anonymous, next to the sea
in one of these tumbledown terraces,

a view at one extreme and a garage
at the other, discarded bottles,
a family in pyjamas in a basement flat

huddled around a TV, seagulls shrieking.
I would celebrate
all lack of aspiration. Who cares

if the windows jam, there are no red geraniums?
Nearby there is everything – post office, museum,
library, park, oceans of tables at restaurants.

I would find myself, I know I would,
eating chips out of paper on a bench
along the seafront, focussing

on the sliver of calm, that silver line
where the grey sky meets the green sea
and the world either ends or begins.

WHAT WE DO

We don't exactly wake
as lie all night in the heat,
eyes open, shifting in dream.

We don't exactly rise
as guide our legs over the side
of the bed, lower our weighty feet.

We don't exactly dress
but put on swimsuits
bathed in moonlight, don't wash

but splash the ocean
over our sweaty faces,
don't dry what's best left

to the air. We don't eat
but we drink lots of water.
We are not so much ourselves

as strangers come to visit,
not fitting but falling
into a foreign location.

We flicker through nights
and days and nights
like a whisper.

A NIGHT LIKE THIS

Curtainlight, TV light, light
of small warm rooms, I pass our old house,
glimpse a bookcase and a tall plant, nothing more.

There's something of me trapped in there,
behind the climbing roses and the freshly painted door,
scratching, itching, beckoning some nights

like after a swim at the Y when you've got to keep
stretching and gasping for air.
Carlight, streetlight, moonlight

down crescents of pillared homes,
terraces, neat and trim, the shops
along Camden Road that spin cocoons

to re-emerge. Once a stranger
but maybe less so on a night
like this. Lacelight, longlight,

all the lights ahead that light
whatever you're searching for, whatever
sooner or later you're bound to find.

LOST LAKE

Who lost this lake, and how?
Mountains overlooking and these pines around.
Its depths and dark go far, its cold
all silvery. A man in a canoe, he could be you,
his paddle poised to plunge. Already I hear
echoes through the trees and up the summit.

Autumn has come but Lost Lake stays
the same. I hate the chill. The sky wakes late,
the sun is weak. I say, Live by your lake.
You could slip in one end
and not ever reach the other. You could swim
to your heart's desire, then lose your breath.

Rocks on a shore – there's a shore.
And in the distance, more explorers.
Or maybe shelter. Nothing urgent here, just the pull
of the sheen on water, the expansive azure sky.
Maybe some poor soul struggled
and was found – if you believe in finding.

LAGOON

for Jean Schuster (1921-1996)

As if you could take a patch of light
and place it on water – spotlight

of moonlight, rippling lagoon-light
the silence of egrets, of heron.

I have carried it along the eastern seaboard
from a lake in upstate New York, where

children watched fires in summer,
ran barefoot under shooting stars,

and from a wood in Massapequa, Long Island,
at the bend before traffic lights,

children bicycled in straw hats, balanced
fishing rods across handlebars,

imagined the Mississippi. Eventually
it alights here, where palm trees

adorn either bank, though in darkness
only the fiery ripples can be seen

dancing and dancing, as if
they could ever extinguish themselves.

PAINTING ENGLAND

See the cows grazing in the valley?

      Velvet brown, heads down, beige brush-tails flicking?

Cluster of trees behind, hills rising beyond, then

      more green and the thinnest divide of land and sky,

wisps of cirrus through a bolt of light.

      Now just in view, the ocean – striations of blue

hugging the horizon. All paths lead there.

      And people are out walking in the sun

this August morning, boats mere dots and this

      meandering river. Notes are drifting in the air –

someone in the distance is laughing, and again

      I am love struck, just as in the beginning.

BIOGRAPHICAL NOTE

Mara Bergman grew up in Wantagh, New York, and graduated from the State University of New York at Oneonta. During her third year, she studied at Goldsmiths College and later made her home in the UK.

Mara's poetry has been published widely here and abroad. Her collection *The Tailor's Three Sons and Other New York Poems* won the *Mslexia* Poetry Pamphlet Competition and was published by Seren in 2015. In 2016, *Crossing Into Tamil Nadu* won a Templar Quarterly Pamphlet Competition. Her poems have been awarded prizes in the Troubadour competition and the Kent & Sussex Open Competition, among others.

Mara works in London as an editor and is also an award-winning author of more than twenty books for young children. She lives with her husband in Tunbridge Wells and has three grown-up children.

www.marabergman.com